Celebrate Recovery®

Living Out the Message of Christ

The Journey Continues

Participant's Guide 8

John Baker is the founder of Celebrate Recovery®, a ministry started at Saddleback Church. It is estimated that over the last 25 years more than 1.5 million people have gone through this Christ-centered recovery program. There are currently over 27,000 churches that have weekly Celebrate Recovery meetings.

John has been on staff since Celebrate Recovery started. He has served as the Pastor of Membership, the Pastor of Ministries, and is currently the Pastor of Saddleback Church's Signature Ministries. He is also serving as one of the nine Elder Pastors at Saddleback. John is a nationally known speaker and trainer in helping churches start Celebrate Recovery ministries.

John's writing accomplishments include Celebrate Recovery's *The Journey Begins* Curriculum, *Life's Healing Choices*, the *Celebrate Recovery Study Bible* (general editor), and *The Landing* and *Celebration Place* (coauthor). John's newest books are *Your First Step to Celebrate Recovery* and *The Celebrate Recovery Devotional* (coauthor).

John and his wife Cheryl, the cofounder of Celebrate Recovery, have been married for more than four decades and have served together in Celebrate Recovery since the beginning. They have two adult children, Laura and Johnny, and five grandchildren.

Johnny Baker has been on staff at Celebrate Recovery since 2004 and has been the Pastor of Celebrate Recovery at Saddleback Church since 2012. As an adult child of an alcoholic who chose to become an alcoholic himself, Johnny is passionate about breaking the cycle of dysfunction in his family and helping other families find the tools that will lead to healing and openness. He knows that because of Jesus Christ, and by continuing to stay active in Celebrate Recovery, Maggie, Chloe, and Jimmy—his three children—will never see him drink. Johnny is a nationally recognized speaker, trainer, and teacher of Celebrate Recovery. He is a coauthor of the *Celebrate Recovery Daily Devotional*, *Celebration Place*, and *The Landing*, and is an associate editor of the *Celebrate Recovery Study Bible*. He has been married since 2000 to his wife Jeni, who serves alongside him in Celebrate Recovery.

Celebrate Recovery®

Living Out the Message of Christ

PARTICIPANT'S GUIDE 8

The Journey Continues

NEW CURRICULUM!

A recovery program based on eight principles from the Beatitudes

JOHN BAKER & JOHNNY BAKER

FOREWORD BY RICK WARREN

ZONDERVAN®

ZONDERVAN

Living Out the Message of Christ

This title is also available as a Zondervan ebook.

Requests for information should be addressed to:
Zondervan, 3900 *Sparks Dr. SE, Grand Rapids, Michigan 49546*

ISBN 978-0-310-13152-6 (softcover)
ISBN 978-0-310-13153-3 (ebook)

Cover design: Brand Navigation
Cover photography: 123rf.com

First Printing May 2016 / Printed in the United States of America

Contents

Foreword

The best known ministry at Saddleback Church—that is going to last for easily 100, maybe 200 years—started when a guy, who was a drunk, came to me with a 13-page letter. And that ministry is called Celebrate Recovery®.

Now, let me just put this in perspective. This may be Saddleback's greatest contribution to the world. Over 20,000 people have completed the step studies at Saddleback's Celebrate Recovery. Over three and a half million people worldwide have gone through a Celebrate Recovery step study.

Right now, around the world, 27,000 churches are using Saddleback's ministry called Celebrate Recovery—27,000 churches! It is so successful that Celebrate Recovery is the official recovery program in 44 state and federal prison systems. It has been translated into 20 different languages.

Do you think John Baker, when he came to see me in my office many years ago and said, "I've got an idea for a ministry, Pastor Rick," imagined it would be affecting three and a half million people in 27,000 churches? No. You have no idea what God wants to do through you. You may have the next big ministry idea. You may have the next Celebrate Recovery dwelling in you—a ministry that could be started and reproduced to bless the whole world. One guy, out of his own pain, starts a ministry that now affects tens of thousands of churches and millions of people.

Rick Warren

(Excerpted from Pastor Warren's talk at Angel Stadium on Saddleback's 35th anniversary)

INTRODUCTION

Don't stop now!

In the final lessons of *The Journey Continues*, you will continue on the road to recovery and live out the rest of your life. This is so much more than maintenance! As in *The Journey Begins*, you'll focus on what God wants to do through you now that you've found even more victory over your hurts, hang-ups, and habits.

In the next few weeks you'll strengthen some healthy habits you began developing in *The Journey Begins.* You'll reinforce the habits of daily time spent with God through journaling, Bible reading, and prayer, as well as taking a daily inventory—and see how these habits can help you build a strong relapse prevention plan.

You'll also take a close look at what God wants to do through you to help other people find the freedom and victory you have found. By giving back to God and saying "yes" to service, you'll have the opportunity to become a Celebrate Recovery leader to help other people go through *The Journey Begins* and *The Journey Continues.*

This is an exciting time in recovery! Get ready, God is about to do some amazing things in, and through, your life as you complete *The Journey Continues.*

John Baker
Johnny Baker

The Road to Recovery

Eight Principles Based on the Beatitudes

By Pastor Rick Warren

1. **R**ealize I'm not God. I admit that I am powerless to control my tendency to do the wrong thing and that my life is unmanageable. (Step 1)
   "Happy are those who know that they are spiritually poor."
   (Matthew 5:3)
2. **E**arnestly believe that God exists, that I matter to Him, and that He has the power to help me recover. (Step 2)
   "Happy are those who mourn, for they shall be comforted."
   (Matthew 5:4)
3. **C**onsciously choose to commit all my life and will to Christ's care and control. (Step 3)
   "Happy are the meek." (Matthew 5:5)
4. **O**penly examine and confess my faults to myself, to God, and to someone I trust. (Steps 4 and 5)
   "Happy are the pure in heart." (Matthew 5:8)
5. **V**oluntarily submit to any and all changes God wants to make in my life and humbly ask Him to remove my character defects. (Steps 6 and 7)
   "Happy are those whose greatest desire is to do what God requires." (Matthew 5:6)
6. **E**valuate all my relationships. Offer forgiveness to those who have hurt me and make amends for harm I've done to others when possible, except when to do so would harm them or others. (Steps 8 and 9)
   "Happy are the merciful." (Matthew 5:7)
   "Happy are the peacemakers." (Matthew 5:9)
7. **R**eserve a time with God for self-examination, Bible reading, and prayer in order to know God and His will for my life and to gain the power to follow His will. (Steps 10 and 11)
8. **Y**ield myself to God to be used to bring this Good News to others, both by my example and my words. (Step 12)
   "Happy are those who are persecuted because they do what God requires." (Matthew 5:10)

Twelve Steps and Their Biblical Comparisons*

1. We admitted we were powerless over our addictions and compulsive behaviors, that our lives had become unmanageable. I know that nothing good lives in me, that is, in my sinful nature.

   "For I know that good itself does not dwell in me, that is, in my sinful nature. For I have the desire to do what is good, but I cannot carry it out." (Romans 7:18)

2. We came to believe that a power greater than ourselves could restore us to sanity.

   "For it is God who works in you to will and to act in order to fulfill his good purpose." (Philippians 2:1)

3. We made a decision to turn our lives and our wills over to the care of God.

   "Therefore, I urge you, brothers and sisters, in view of God's mercy, to offer your bodies as a living sacrifice, holy and pleasing to God—this is your true and proper of worship." (Romans 12:1)

4. We made a searching and fearless moral inventory of ourselves.

   "Let us examine our ways and test them, and let us return to the LORD." (Lamentations 3:40)

5. We admitted to God, to ourselves, and to another human being the exact nature of our wrongs.

   "Therefore confess your sins to each other and pray for each other so that you may be healed." (James 5:16)

6. We were entirely ready to have God remove all these defects of character.

   "Humble yourselves before the LORD, and he will lift you up." (James 4:10)

7. We humbly asked Him to remove all our shortcomings.

   "If we confess our sins, he is faithful and will forgive us our sins and purify us from all unrighteousness." (1 John 1:9)

8. We made a list of all persons we had harmed and became willing to make amends to them all.

   "Do to others as you would have them do to you." (Luke 6:31)

9. We made direct amends to such people whenever possible, except when to do so would injure them or others.

   "Therefore, if you are offering your gift at the altar and there remember that your brother or sister has something against you, leave your gift there in front of the altar. First go and be reconciled to them; then come and offer your gift." (Matthew 5:23–24)

10. We continued to take personal inventory and when we were wrong, promptly admitted it.

    "So, if you think you are standing firm, be careful that you don't fall!" (1 Corinthians 10:12)

11. We sought through prayer and meditation to improve our conscious contact with God, praying only for knowledge of His will for us, and power to carry that out.

    "Let the message of Christ dwell among you richly." (Colossians 3:16)

12. Having had a spiritual experience as the result of these steps, we try to carry this message to others and practice these principles in all our affairs.

    "Brothers and sisters, if someone is caught in a sin, you who live by the Spirit should restore that person gently. But watch yourselves, or you also may be tempted." (Galatians 6:1)

* Throughout this material, you will notice several references to the Christ-centered 12 Steps. Our prayer is that Celebrate Recovery will create a bridge to the millions of people who are familiar with the secular 12 Steps (we acknowledge the use of some material from the 12 Suggested Steps of Alcoholics Anonymous) and in so doing, introduce them to the one and only true Higher Power, Jesus Christ. Once they begin that relationship, asking Christ into their hearts as Lord and Savior, true healing and recovery can begin!

Serenity Prayer

God, grant me the serenity
to accept the things I cannot change,
the courage to change the things I can,
and the wisdom to know the difference.
Living one day at a time,
enjoying one moment at a time;
accepting hardship as a pathway to peace;
taking, as Jesus did,
this sinful world as it is,
not as I would have it;
trusting that You will make all things right
if I surrender to Your will;
so that I may be reasonably happy in this life
and supremely happy with You forever in the next.
Amen.

Reinhold Niebuhr

Celebrate Recovery's Small Group Guidelines

The following five guidelines will ensure that your small group is a safe place. They need to be read at the beginning of every meeting.

1. Keep your sharing focused on your own thoughts and feelings. Limit your sharing to three to five minutes.
2. There is NO cross talk. Cross talk is when two individuals engage in conversation excluding all others. Each person is free to express his or her feelings without interruptions.
3. We are here to support one another, not "fix" another.
4. Anonymity and confidentiality are basic requirements. What is shared in the group stays in the group. The only exception is when someone threatens to injure themselves or others.
5. Offensive language has no place in a Christ-centered recovery group.

Lesson 19

Habits

Principle 7: Reserve a daily time with God for self-examination, Bible reading, and prayer in order to know God and His will for my life and to gain the power to follow His will.

Step 10: We continued to take personal inventory and when we were wrong, promptly admitted it.

"So if you think you are standing firm, be careful that you don't fall!" (1 Corinthians 10:12)

Please begin your time together by reading "The Tenth Step, Day 270" from the *Celebrate Recovery Daily Devotional.*

In Celebrate Recovery, we often talk about breaking bad habits. But recovery is more than stopping old, negative behaviors; it's also about starting new, healthy ones. In Principle 7, we see how we are to begin living out our lives; we "reserve a daily time with God for self-examination, Bible reading, and prayer in order to know God and His will for my life and to gain the power to follow His will."

Principle 7 is all about the daily habits we form so that we can walk in step with God for the remainder of our lives. We've done some great work in dealing with the pain in our pasts, and have continued in the process of doing our part to make our relationships healthy. Now we see how we can do what Jesus told us to do in John 15:5: "I am the vine; you are the branches. If you remain in me and I in you, you will bear much fruit; apart from me you can do nothing."

Principle 7 gives us three daily habits that help us remain in Jesus.

Habit #1: Self-examination

> *"Search me, God, and know my heart; test me and know my anxious thoughts. See if there is any offensive way in me, and lead me in the way everlasting." (Psalm 139:23–24)*

Just because we have completed a moral inventory doesn't mean we don't still need to examine our motives and our actions. As we will see in the next lesson, a daily inventory is vital to our continued growth. The best tool for self-examination is a journal. A journal helps us remember where we have been and to see what God is doing in our lives. It allows us to go back in time and clearly recount all of the ways we have changed.

In *The Journey Begins* you were introduced to the idea of journaling and even had a seven-day challenge to help you kick-start this habit. If you completed that exercise and kept at it, congratulations! You have undoubtedly recorded great insights and growth. You have learned things about yourself and seen things in writing that you may not have realized were true. If you were less successful in that first attempt, make this the time to get started! There are so many ways to do this daily habit. You can pick up a *Celebrate Recovery Journal*, a spiral-bound notebook, or any one of the many journaling apps available. It doesn't matter how you journal; the important thing is that you do it!

If you are struggling with this habit, go back to Lesson 19 of *The Journey Begins* for helpful tips on how to get started.

> *"Look to the LORD and his strength; seek his face always. Remember the wonders he has done, his miracles, and the judgments he pronounced." (1 Chronicles 16:11–12)*

> *"Let us examine our ways and test them, and let us return to the LORD." (Lamentations 3:40)*

Habit #2: Bible Reading

"Your word is a lamp for my feet, a light on my path."
(Psalm 119:105)

Going to God's Word daily is one of the most important habits any follower of Jesus can build into his or her life. The Bible has been called God's love letter to us and God's instruction manual for life. The Bible is a firsthand account of what God can do in the lives of those who trust in Him. Again, this is a habit you may have already formed. If so, keep it up. If you haven't, begin today. Start by reading for a few minutes a day and see how God speaks to you through His Word.

Just as with journaling, there are many tools to help you start, or grow in, this daily habit. You can use the *Celebrate Recovery Bible*, a different Bible, or an app like YouVersion. Again, the important thing is to make daily reading God's Word a part of your life.

"But grow in the grace and knowledge of our Lord
and Savior Jesus Christ. To him be glory both
now and forever! Amen." (2 Peter 3:18)

"I reach out for your commands, which I love, that I
may meditate on your decrees." (Psalm 119:48)

Habit #3: Prayer

"Devote yourselves to prayer, being watchful and thankful."
(Colossians 4:2)

Many people have the wrong idea about prayer. They think praying is all about talking. They begin their time praying, asking God for His will and for His answers, and say "amen" without taking the time to listen for His response! Imagine if we treated each other like that! How would you feel if you had a friend who called you on the phone, talked for twenty minutes, and then hung up before you had a chance to speak? Chances are you wouldn't expect that friend to know you very well.

When we talk to God in prayer, we need to make sure we are giving Him time to talk back to us. Now, God may never talk audibly to you (He never has to me—Johnny), but He may speak to you through a feeling (you sense what He wants you to do) or through leading you by His Spirit. The point is: go to God in prayer, daily, asking Him to meet your needs, thanking Him for what He's done, and asking Him for His will. Then make sure you take the time to allow Him to speak back to you! His answer may not be immediate; He may even speak through a friend or accountability partner, so we need to continue to go to Him with an open heart and listen for His guidance.

"Answer me when I call to you, my righteous God. Give me relief from my distress; have mercy on me and hear my prayer." (Psalm 4:1)

"Do not be anxious about anything, but in every situation, by prayer and petition, with thanksgiving, present your requests to God." (Philippians 4:6)

"I call on you, my God, for you will answer me; turn your ear to me and hear my prayer." (Psalm 17:6)

There are other habits to form that will help us live out our recovery journey and continue on the pathway Jesus has set before us, but these three habits are a good place to begin. This week, try to begin building, or continue building, these three habits into your life. As you do, take note of what God is doing in your life through these habits.

Questions for Reflection and Discussion

1. Which one of these habits is strongest in your life? How did you go about building and growing this habit?

2. Which of these habits is the weakest in your life? What steps do you need to take to build it up?

3. Do you currently journal? If not, how will you get started? If you do journal, what are some lessons you have learned about your recovery through this habit?

4. Do you have a daily time reading God's Word? If not, how will you get started? If you do, what is the last thing God showed you through His Word?

5. Have you ever memorized a Bible verse? What's the last verse you committed to memory, and how has it been meaningful to you?

6. How often do you pray? When you pray, do you regularly slow down long enough for God to speak?

7. What's the last thing you "heard" from God? (Remember, this may not be an audible voice.)

8. How would daily implementing these habits affect your recovery?

9. Will you commit to building, or strengthening, these habits this week? Who will you ask to keep you accountable?

Prayer

Father, thank You that Celebrate Recovery isn't just about breaking bad habits, but it's also about starting new, healthy ones. Help me this week as I continue building these habits into my life. Show me ways to journal, read my Bible, and pray more this week. I ask that these three habits would strengthen my recovery, but more importantly that they'd draw me closer to You. In Your name I pray, amen.

Lesson 20

Daily Inventory

Principle 7: Reserve a daily time with God for self-examination, Bible reading, and prayer in order to know God and His will for my life and to gain the power to follow His will.

Step 10: We continued to take personal inventory and when we were wrong, promptly admitted it.

"So, if you think you are standing firm, be careful that you don't fall!" (1 Corinthians 10:12)

Please begin your time together by reading "Clear Mind, Clean Heart, Day 75" from the *Celebrate Recovery Daily Devotional.*

In this lesson, we want to focus on the first part of Principle 7, "Reserve a daily time with God for self-examination . . ."

Journaling

Hopefully, you have continued making journaling a daily habit. With this habit, you have continued to commit to recapping your day in written form—the good and the bad, the successes and the times when you made mistakes.

If for some reason, you have stopped journaling, please pray about starting it again. You may be thinking that you don't have time to journal. The truth is, you don't have time not too!

Remember the two reasons why journaling is a key part to each of our recoveries as we continue the journey:

1. When you write down areas in which you owe amends, it will help you to be aware of unhealthy patterns that may be developing. As you identify them, you can work on them with the help of Jesus Christ and your sponsor and accountability partner/team.
2. You can keep the amends you owe to a very "short list." As soon as you write down an issue, you can make a plan to *promptly* offer your amends. After you make the amends, you can cross it off in your journal.

Inventory

Please remember as we refocus on Step 10 and Principle 7, we continue the journey of applying what we have discovered in the first nine steps.

We humbly live daily, in reality, not denial. We have done our best to amend our past. Through God's guidance, we can make healing choices about the emotions that affect our thinking and actions. And best of all, we can start to take *action*, positive action, instead of constant *reaction* to the issues we face daily.

God has provided us with a daily checklist for our new lifestyle. It's called the "Great Commandment," and it is found in Matthew 22:37–40 where Jesus said, " 'Love the Lord your God with all your heart ... soul and ... mind.' This is the first and greatest commandment. And the second is like it: 'Love your neighbor as yourself.' All the Law and the Prophets hang on these two commandments."

Step 10—"We continued to take personal inventory and when we were wrong, promptly admitted it"—does not say how often to take an inventory, but remember the three suggestions *The Journey Begins* offered to help us keep on the right road, God's road to recovery.

1. Do an ongoing inventory.

You can keep an ongoing inventory throughout the day. The best time to admit you are wrong is the exact time that you are made aware of it. Why wait?

2. Do a daily inventory.

At the end of each day, you can look over your daily activities, searching where you might have harmed someone or where you acted out of anger or fear. But remember to keep your daily inventory balanced by also including the things that you did right that day. After all, at this point in your recovery you are doing more things right than wrong! The best way to do this is to journal.

3. Do a periodic inventory.

Take a periodic inventory about every three months. Get away on a "mini retreat"! Bring your daily journal with you, and pray as you read through the last ninety days of your journal entries. Ask God to show you areas in your life that you can improve on in the next ninety days and celebrate the victories that you have made.

By continuing to take, or recommitting to an ongoing, a daily, and a periodic inventory, we can work Step 10 to the best of our abilities. With God's help, we can keep our side of the street clean.

Here are a few key verses to follow for Principle 7:

"The hearts of the wise make their mouths prudent, and their lips promote instruction." (Proverbs 16:23)

"Do not let any unwholesome talk come out of your mouths, but only what is helpful for building others up according to their needs, that it may benefit those who listen." (Ephesians 4:29)

"The wise in heart are called discerning, and gracious words promote instruction." (Proverbs 16:21)

"Anxiety weighs down the heart, but a kind word cheers it up." (Proverbs 12:25)

"If I speak in the tongues of men or of angels, but do not have love, I am only a resounding gong or a clanging cymbal." (1 Corinthians 13:1)

Step 10 Daily Action Plan

1. Continue to take an ongoing and daily inventory, and when you are wrong, promptly make your amends.
2. Summarize the events of your day in your journal.
3. Read and memorize one of the Principle 7 verses listed above.
4. Live out all the steps and principles to the best of your ability.

The key verse for this lesson is Mark 14:38: "Watch and pray so that you do not fall into temptation. The spirit is willing, but the body is weak."

Questions for Reflection and Discussion

1. How are you doing with your habit of journaling? Do you journal daily? Once a week? Or not at all?

2. If you are not journaling daily, why not?

3. What are some of the benefits you have received from doing an ongoing inventory?

4. What are some of the benefits you have received from doing a daily inventory?

5. What are some of the benefits you have received from doing a periodic inventory? Where do you get away to?

6. How about those you sponsor? Have you helped them learn the key differences of the three types of inventories? Do you spend time reviewing their periodic inventories?

Prayer

Dear God, thank You for today. Thank You for giving me the tools to continue to work my program and live my life differently, centered in Your will. Lord, help me to make my amends promptly and ask for forgiveness. In all my relationships, help me to do my part in making them healthy and growing. In Jesus' name I pray, amen.

Lesson 21

RELAPSE

Principle 7: Reserve a daily time with God for self-examination, Bible reading, and prayer in order to know God and His will for my life and to gain the power to follow His will.

Step 11: We sought through prayer and meditation to improve our conscious contact with God, praying only for knowledge of His will for us, and power to carry that out.

"Let the message of Christ dwell among you richly."
(Colossians 3:16)

Please begin your time together by reading "The Eleventh Step, Day 300" from the *Celebrate Recovery Daily Devotional.*

One of the realities of recovery is that relapse is possible. Many think relapse is unavoidable. That is simply not true. Relapse is preventable if precautions are taken. If you have made it this far through *The Journey Continues*, you have done a great job! You have found some freedom and victory over major issues and character defects in your life. Now is the time to protect what you have obtained.

Important Note:

If you have relapsed, you may be feeling the desire to pull away from your group or to run away from God. Resist this temptation! Now is the time to draw close to the people in your group and to Jesus. The enemy wants you to stay stuck and to go back to your hurts, hang-ups, and habits, but Jesus wants you to be free. So, if you have relapsed and are beating yourself up, remember the words of Romans 8:1, "Therefore, there is now no condemnation for those who are in Christ Jesus"!

Learn from this experience and allow God to do something new inside of you; don't allow it to push you away.

—Johnny Baker

RELAPSE

How do you protect your recovery? By setting up a RELAPSE prevention plan. A good plan will allow you to:

R—Recognize your weak points

Everyone has strengths and weaknesses in his or her life. In your group, some people are further along in their recovery and some are people are not as far along. Your experiences vary greatly. Because of this, you each have unique challenges to maintaining, and growing in, your own recovery journey. Some people know they are more susceptible to relapse when they are alone, or when they are sad, or when they are angry. The key is to know when you are at your most vulnerable. Once you recognize your weak points, you will be able to protect yourself when you are triggered to act out.

And remember, just because we all have weak points doesn't mean we are doomed to relapse. Why? Because God has the power to see us through!

"He gives strength to the weary and increases the power of the weak." (Isaiah 40:29)

"Search me, God, and know my heart; test me and know my anxious thoughts. See if there is any offensive way in me, and lead me in the way everlasting." (Psalm 139:23–24)

E—Establish escape routes

While relapse is preventable, temptation is not. If you have taken the time to recognize your weak points, you now know when temptation is most likely to come. But being tempted to relapse isn't the same thing as actually relapsing. Temptation means it's time to put your guard up. Instead of rolling over and giving in to the impulse to act out, temptation is a call to action! When you are tempted, the first thing to do is to look for an escape route. If the temptation is there, God has also provide a way to escape it.

"No temptation has overtaken you except what is common to mankind. And God is faithful; he will not let you be tempted beyond what you can bear. But when you are tempted, he will also provide a way out so that you can endure it." (1 Corinthians 10:13)

L—Listen to your support team

Your sponsor and accountability partners/team, and the members of this group, know things about you that you may not even know yourself. Have you ever had the experience of someone asking you what's wrong before you even spoke? That person knew your cues, your expressions, your body language; in short, they knew you well enough to know something was wrong. In the same way, the people in your group have been with you a long time now. They have seen your good days and bad days. If someone on your support team calls you or talks to you and says they feel you are flirting with relapse, listen to them. They may see something you are having trouble identifying.

"Therefore encourage one another and build each other up, just as in fact you are doing." (1 Thessalonians 5:11)

"As iron sharpens iron, so one person sharpens another." (Proverbs 27:17)

A—Acknowledge your level of risk

You may not realize it, but you might already be on the path to relapse! As discussed above, this does not mean that you must give in, but you need to be aware of your risk level. The following information, called "The Predictable Pattern of Relapse" comes from *Life's Healing Choices:*

Phase 1: Complacency

Relapse begins when we get comfortable. We've confessed our problem, we've started dealing with it, and we've made some progress. Then we get comfortable, and one day we stop praying about it, and then we stop working at it. Our pain level has been reduced—not eliminated but reduced—and we think we can live with the reduced level of pain. We haven't thoroughly dealt with our problem, but we don't feel as desperate about it as we once did. We think we don't need to meet with our support group anymore. We don't need to work the choices anymore. We don't need to call our accountability partner anymore. And before we know it, we have become complacent.

Phase 2: Confusion

In this phase we begin to rationalize and play mental games with ourselves. We say things like, "Maybe my problem really wasn't all that bad; maybe I can handle it by myself." We forget how bad it used to be. Reality becomes fuzzy and confused, and we think we can control our problems by ourselves.

(cont.)

Phase 3: Compromise

When we get to this phase, we go back to the place of temptation. We return to the risky situation that got us in the first place, whether it's the bar, the mall, 31 Flavors, or that "XXX" Internet site. We go back to that unsafe place like the gambler who says, "Let's go to Vegas and just see the shows." But when we place ourselves in risky situations, we'll likely make poor choices. It may begin with little things, but it won't be long before it all unravels and all the ground that's been gained is lost. That brings us to Phase 4.

Phase 4: Catastrophe

This is when we actually give in to the old hurt, old hang-up, or old habit. The hate comes back, the resentment returns, or we fall back into the old patterns of behavior. But we need to understand this: the catastrophe is not the relapse. The relapse began in Phase 1 with complacency.

To avoid the catastrophe of relapse, we need to take the time to see if we fit somewhere in this pattern, and if so, take action.

"Let us examine our ways and test them, and let us return to the LORD." (Lamentations 3:40)

"The crucible for silver and the furnace for gold, but the LORD tests the heart." (Proverbs 17:3)

"Watch and pray so that you will not fall into temptation. The spirit is willing, but the flesh is weak." (Matthew 26:41)

P—Pray and read your Bible daily

We have already looked at prayer and Bible reading as habits that will help keep us growing, but they are essential tools for avoiding relapse as well. Prayer connects us to God; it keeps us in step with Him. Bible reading gives us insight into what God wants for us. They are essential tools in any relapse prevention plan.

"In the same way, the Spirit helps us in our weakness. We do not know what we ought to pray for, but the Spirit himself intercedes for us through wordless groans." (Romans 8:26)

"I will remember the deeds of the LORD; yes, I will remember your miracles of long ago. I will consider all your works and meditate on all your mighty deeds." (Psalm 77:11–12)

S—Serve others, especially the newcomers

One of the best ways to protect our recoveries is by serving other people. Remember, the way to ensure service is done in a non-codependent way is to keep our focus on Christ. Serving others, which we will discuss in detail in later lessons, protects our recoveries in several ways.

- It takes the focus off us and puts it onto other people.
- It gives our pain a purpose.
- It reminds us where we were when we first started, and shows us how far we've come.
- It gives us a way to directly serve Jesus and to thank Him for what He's done for us.

"Whoever tries to keep their life will lose it, and whoever loses their life will preserve it." (Luke 17:33)

"Serve wholeheartedly, as if you were serving the Lord, not people." (Ephesians 6:7)

"You, my brothers and sisters, were called to be free. But do not use your freedom to indulge the flesh; rather, serve one another humbly in love." (Galatians 5:13)

E—Enjoy the victories you have been given

There is one tool for avoiding relapse that often goes unnoticed, and that is enjoying the victory we have been given. Remember, this program is called *Celebrate* Recovery! We need to enjoy the victories God has been giving us. By this point in our recovery, it is likely we have more good days than bad ones. We need to enjoy that victory! We are more likely to protect the things we enjoy and celebrate. So if we have found even small victories, we need to enjoy them!

"A cheerful heart is good medicine, but a crushed spirit dries up the bones." (Proverbs 17:22)

"Nevertheless, I will bring health and healing to it; I will heal my people and will let them enjoy abundant peace and security." (Jeremiah 33:6)

Questions for Reflection and Discussion

1. How have you protected yourself from relapse in the past?

2. If you have relapsed, what would you like others to learn from your experience?

3. What are some of your weak points? Be specific.

4. How do you escape temptation?

5. Who has the ability to ask you tough questions or to speak truth into your life?

6. Are you on "The Predictable Pattern of Relapse" right now? If so, where? And how will you protect your recovery in light of this discovery?

7. How has daily prayer and Bible reading strengthened your recovery?

8. Who and where are you serving today? How has serving the newcomer reminded you of what life was like when you first started recovery?

9. How are you enjoying the victories you have been given? How do you *celebrate* your recovery?

Prayer

Heavenly Father, thank You for the victories You have given me. Help me protect them by preparing a plan to avoid relapse. Father, I don't want to go back to my old hurts, hang-ups, or habits. Help me to keep growing and moving forward, creating new, positive habits in my life. Help keep me in step with You. It's in Your name I pray, Jesus. Amen.

Lesson 22

GRATITUDE

Principle 7: Reserve a daily time with God for self-examination, Bible reading, and prayer in order to know God and His will for my life and to gain the power to follow His will.

Step 11: We sought through prayer and meditation to improve our conscious contact with God, praying only for knowledge of His will for us and power to carry that out.

"Let the message of Christ dwell among you richly."
(Colossians 3:16)

Please begin your time together by reading "Active Gratitude, Day 130" from the *Celebrate Recovery Daily Devotional.*

In Principle 7, we began to focus our attention outwardly rather than inwardly. As we continue our journey, as we continue to grow in our conscious contact with God, He begins to unfold in our lives. The way we do this, according to Principle 7, is to "reserve a daily time with God." During this time, we focus on Him by praying and meditating.

Prayer is talking to God. Meditation is listening to God on a daily basis. Meditation doesn't mean we get into some yoga-type position or murmur, "om, om, om." We simply focus on, and think about, God or a certain Scripture verse or maybe even just one or two words. This week, try to focus on just one word: *gratitude.*

By this point in our journey, we have learned to listen to God, who tells us that we have great worth. We have learned that if we start our day with Principle 7 and end it by doing our daily inventories, we can have a pretty good day—a reasonably happy day. This is one way we choose to live "one day at a time" and one way we can continue to help prevent relapse.

We have learned a great way to prevent relapse and struggles in our recoveries is by maintaining an "attitude of gratitude."

Gratitude

This week, it doesn't matter how many years of recovery we have, we all need to allow our prayers to be focused on our gratitude in four key areas of our lives: God, others, recovery growth, and church.

As always, we need to write them down on our "Gratitude List" (pages 43–46). If you haven't written a gratitude list in a while, feel free to go back as far as six months or even a year as you complete this new list. Continue to add new items to this list as God brings them to mind this week. (**Note:** Be sure to complete your list prior to your meeting so everyone has time to share! Your responses will be the focus of group discussion; there are no "Questions for Reflection and Discussion" this time.)

Using your gratitude list, daily living out Principle 7, making your recovery meetings a priority, and getting involved in service are the best ways to prevent relapse.

Gratitude List

First, gratitude toward God

"Do not be anxious about anything, but in everything, by prayer and petition, with thanksgiving, present your requests to God." (Philippians 4:6)

"Give thanks to the LORD for his unfailing love and his wonderful deeds for mankind!" (Psalm 107:15)

What are at least two areas of your life in which you can see God's hand for which you are grateful?

1.

2.

Second, gratitude for others

Second, list the individuals that God has placed in your life to walk alongside you on your road of recovery.

"Let the peace of Christ rule in your hearts, since as members of one body you were called to peace. And be thankful. Let the message of Christ dwell among you richly as you teach and admonish one another with all wisdom through psalms, hymns, and songs from the Spirit, singing to God with gratitude in your hearts."
(Colossians 3:15–16)

Who are you grateful for? Why? List at least two individuals.

1.

2.

Third, your recovery thus far

The third area you can be grateful for is the months or years of your recovery.

> *"Therefore, since we are surrounded by such a great cloud of witnesses, let us throw off everything that hinders and the sin that so easily entangles. And let us run with perseverance the race marked out for us, fixing our eyes on Jesus, the pioneer and perfecter of faith. For the joy set before him he endured the cross, scorning its shame, and sat down at the right hand of the throne of God. Consider him who endured such opposition from sinners, so that you will not grow weary and lose heart." (Hebrews 12:1–3)*

What are two recent growth areas of your recovery for which you are thankful? Why?

1.

2.

Fourth, your church family

The fourth area to be grateful for is your church for being a safe place and providing Celebrate Recovery.

"Enter his gates with thanksgiving and his courts with praise; give thanks to him and praise his name. For the LORD is good and his love endures forever; his faithfulness continues through all generations." (Psalm 100:4–5)

What are two specific areas of your church for which you are grateful? Why?

1.

2.

Prayer

Dear God, help me set aside all the hassles and noise of the world to focus on and listen just to You for the next few minutes. Help me get to know You better. Help me to better understand Your plan, Your purpose for my life. Father, help me live within today, seeking Your will and living this day as You would have me to live.

It is my prayer to have others see me as Yours, not just in my words but, more importantly, in my actions. Thank You for Your love, Your grace, and Your perfect forgiveness. Thank You for all of those You have placed in my life, for my program, my recovery, and my church family. Your will be done, not mine. In Your Son's name I pray, amen.

Lesson 23

GIVE

Principle 8: Yield myself to God to be used to bring this Good News to others, both by my example and my words.

"Happy are those who are persecuted because they do what God requires." (Matthew 5:10)

Step 12: Having had a spiritual experience as the result of these steps, we try to carry this message to others, and practice these principles in all our affairs.

"Brothers and sisters, if someone is caught in a sin, you who live by the Spirit should restore that person gently. But watch yourselves, or you also may be tempted." (Galatians 6:1)

Please begin your time together by reading "The Twelfth Step, Day 330" from the *Celebrate Recovery Daily Devotional.*

Principle 8 is all about giving. It's about living out the rest of our lives in service—service to Christ and service to others. That's what it means to "yield myself to God." It means that we start looking for ways to give back, to God and to others, what we have received. In *The Journey Begins* we looked at what it means to GIVE, but now we will look at what we have to offer to others in service.

GIVE

G—Gifts

We have each received God-given gifts. He has shaped each of us in order to serve Him and His people. In Celebrate Recovery, we all have at least two God-given gifts in common. First, He has given us the gift of His grace when we each accepted Jesus as our Lord and Savior. Second, we each have received the gift of victory over particular hurts, hang-ups, and habits. While much of our individual journeys may look very different, we have at least those two gifts in common.

But God has also gifted each of us in many unique ways. You may not feel particularly gifted, but the Bible says God has specially gifted each of us. Many books have written about spiritual gifts. For our purposes, know two things: (1) God has gifted you, and (2) He wants you to use your gifts to help other people. We are not supposed to keep our gifts to ourselves!

"We have different gifts, according to the grace given to each of us. If your gift is prophesying, then prophesy in accordance with your faith; if it is serving, then serve; if it is teaching, then teach; if it is to encourage, then give encouragement; if it is giving, then give generously; if it is to lead, do it diligently; if it is to show mercy, do it cheerfully." (Romans 12:6–8)

"There are different kinds of gifts, but the same Spirit distributes them. There are different kinds of service, but the same Lord." (1 Corinthians 12:4–5)

"Each of you should use whatever gift you have received to serve others, as faithful stewards of God's grace in its various forms." (1 Peter 4:10)

I—Interest

Perhaps the greatest gift we can give other people is our interest. We live in a world clamoring for our attention. Screens shout at us at every opportunity. Never has the temptation to move on to the next thing, or has the fear of missing out, been stronger. We check our social media sites looking for "likes" and "comments" and stories pointing us to the new and the now.

So when we sit down with someone and pay them attention, when we show interest in them, we are giving them something both rare and valuable. Slowing down enough to get to know the people God puts in our path — to listen and give them our time — is a powerful way to give back.

"Do nothing out of selfish ambition or vain conceit. Rather, in humility value others above yourselves, not looking to your own interests but each of you to the interests of the others." (Philippians 2:3–4)

Jesus said, "A new command I give you: Love one another. As I have loved you, so you must love one another. By this everyone will know that you are my disciples, if you love one another." (John 13:34–35)

"Keep on loving one another as brothers and sisters." (Hebrews 13:1)

V — Victories

Another great gift we can give in service is by sharing our victories. We need to remember how we felt when we first started Celebrate Recovery. Most people don't come to Celebrate Recovery for the first time on a good day. Usually people seek out recovery when they are out of options or when their pain exceeds the fear of change. If we can remember how we felt when we first started, we recall that things felt pretty bleak. Of course, your experience may be very different, but you probably never imagined the things God had in store for you when you first started.

By sharing our victories with other people, especially newcomers, we give them a great gift! We let them know that Jesus has the power to help them change and that Celebrate Recovery works! After all, why would anyone stay in a program that never helped anyone? By sharing our victory, by telling other people what Jesus has done and is still doing for us, we are telling them that God has changed us, little by little and day by day. We also are telling them that God can do it for them too!

"Sing to him, sing praise to him; tell of all his wonderful acts." (Psalm 105:2)

He replied, "... One thing I do know. I was blind but now I see!" (John 9:25)

E—Encouragement

Encouragement goes hand-in-hand with sharing victories. When we share our victories we show people that change is possible, because it happened to us. When we meet people who are just beginning their recovery journey, or who feel like giving up, we can encourage them to keep going. We can tell them that God isn't finished with them yet.

With a simple phone call, text, or face-to-face conversation, we can give others the gift of encouragement. We can be there when they are going through hard times. We can hold them when they are hurting, and we can hold them up when they feel that they can't go on.

"Being confident of this, that he who began a good work in you will carry it on to completion until the day of Christ Jesus." (Philippians 1:6)

"Let the message of Christ dwell among you richly as you teach and admonish one another with all wisdom through psalms, hymns, and songs from the Spirit, singing to God with gratitude in your hearts." (Colossians 3:16)

Questions for Reflection and Discussion

As you answer the questions this week, try to think of someone you can give back to. Ask God to bring to mind someone you can serve. We have been given so much, it's time to give back.

1. Who do you know that you can give back to this week?

2. What gifts have you been given? Be specific. How can you use these gifts for others?

3. In what ways would those around you say you're gifted?

4. How can you show interest in others?

5. What things keep you from showing your loved ones that you're interested in them?

6. What victory can you share with a newcomer this week?

7. Is there a new victory in your life that you have been keeping to yourself? If so, share it now.

8. Who do you know that you need to encourage? And how can you encourage them?

9. How does sharing your gifts, interest, victories, and encouragement with others give back to God? And what has been keeping you from sharing this way in the past?

Prayer

God, You have given me so much. As I think back to what I was like when I first started Celebrate Recovery, I can barely recognize that person. I have been giving back to others already, but now I commit to take it up a notch. Please show me how I can use my gifts, my interest, my victories, and encouragement to serve other people and to give back to You. I ask You to put people that I can give back to on my path this week. It's in Your name I pray, amen.

Lesson 24

YES

Principle 8: Yield myself to God to be used to bring this Good News to others, both by my example and by my words.

"Happy are those who are persecuted because they do what God requires." (Matthew 5:10)

Step 12: Having had a spiritual experience as the result of these steps, we try to carry this message to others and to practice these principles in all our affairs.

"Brothers and sisters, if someone is caught in a sin, you who live by the Spirit should restore that person gently. But watch yourselves, or you also may be tempted." (Galatians 6:1)

Please begin your time together by reading "The Special Guest, Day 360" from the *Celebrate Recovery Daily Devotional.*

We have used this illustration many times, but it is still relevant today. Take an old, beat-up soda can—dirty, dented, holes in it. A few years ago, it would have been thrown in the garbage and deemed useless, of no value. Today it can be recycled, melted down, purified, and made into a new can—shiny and clean—that can be used again.

In this lesson, we are going to focus on new ways of letting God recycle our pain by allowing God's fire and light to shine on it, to melt down our old hurts, hang-ups, and habits so they can be used again in a positive way.

By working through the steps and principles in *The Journey Begins*, we learned that pain has value, as do the people who experience it. Remember, our brokenness is not useless. God can always use your pain to build a stronger you!

Principle 8 states, "Yield myself to God to be used to bring this Good News to others, both by my example and by my words." To truly practice this principle, we must give God the latitude to use us as He sees fit. We do that by presenting everything we have—our time, talents, and treasures—to Him. We hold loosely all that we call our own, recognizing that all of it comes from His hand.

Our acrostic couldn't be any more positive! It is the word YES.

YES

Y—Yield myself to God and to the service of others

That's what Principle 8 is all about. God has created and gifted each of us with a unique purpose. His purpose, His plan, for us is perfect. All we have to do is to yield ourselves to His will for us.

> *"Then Jesus said to his disciples, 'Whoever wants to be my disciple must deny themselves and take up their cross and follow me.'" (Matthew 16:24)*

> *"Let us hold unswervingly to the hope we profess, for he who promised is faithful. And let us consider how we may spur one another on toward love and good deeds." (Hebrews 10:23–24)*

E—Example is what is important to others

Do they see Christ in you? We must be doers of the Word. We must have a message worth remembering, a lifestyle worth considering, and a faith worth imitating.

"Do not merely listen to the word, and so deceive yourselves. Do what it says." (James 1:22)

"Follow my example, as I follow the example of Christ." (1 Corinthians 11:1)

S—Serve others as Jesus Christ did by finding new ways to help them

We need to use new tools and ways to reach the next generation. But God's message must remain constant and undiluted.

"But now, by dying to what once bound us, we have been released from the law so that we serve in the new way of the Spirit, and not in the old way of the written code." (Romans 7:6)

"There are different kinds of gifts, but the same Spirit distributes them. There are different kinds of service, but the same Lord." (1 Corinthians 12:4–5)

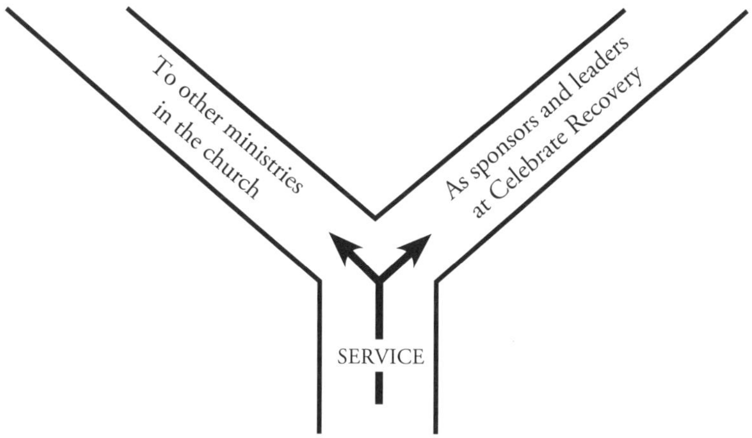

The road to recovery leads to service. When you reach Principle 8, the road splits. Most of you will choose to serve at Celebrate Recovery. Others will choose to serve in other areas of the church. The fact is, both are important.

The greatest need is for you to share your experiences, strengths, and hopes with newcomers at Celebrate Recovery. You do that as leaders, sponsors, and accountability partners. But the church also needs your service. As you serve outside of Celebrate Recovery, you can share with others and encourage them to get them into recovery when they are ready to work on their hurts, hang-ups, and habits.

Questions for Reflection and Discussion

1. In Celebrate Recovery, what areas have you served in? List the dates.

2. From the above list, what were your two most fulfilling and fruitful areas of service? Why?

3. How did your example and actions of service help others start serving as well?

4. If you knew you could choose any way to serve God in Celebrate Recovery—and knew you wouldn't fail—what would it be? What's holding you back?

5. What are some new ways you could reach out to get more newcomers to attend Celebrate Recovery? Be specific.

6. If you are not currently giving back by serving, what's stopping you?

Prayer

Dear Jesus, as it would please You, bring me someone today whom I can serve. Please continue to help me daily choose to make my life a mission, not an intermission. Amen.

If you will pray this prayer every morning, watch how God will use you in ways you never thought possible!

Lesson 25

LEADER

Please begin your time together by reading "Serving Others, Day 302" from the *Celebrate Recovery Daily Devotional.*

In order for Celebrate Recovery to grow and in order for us to "bring this Good News to others," it is important that you become a leader. You have had at least two great leaders, one for this group and one for your *The Journey Begins* step study. Because they stepped across the line and decided to give back by becoming leaders, you had the opportunity to attend these groups. Now it's your turn.

But you might be saying, "Who? Me? I'm not a leader!" That's where you're wrong. It doesn't take a superhero to be a leader. So what are the qualities of a great Celebrate Recovery leader?

LEADER

Celebrate Recovery leaders are:

L—Learners

You may have heard the statement, "Leaders are learners." It's true. Great leaders never stop learning. Think about all of the things you have learned about God and yourself during your time in Celebrate Recovery! You are a learner! To continue in the process of learning, you now have the opportunity to repeat the process, as a leader of *The Journey Begins* and eventually *The Journey Continues.* You can help others learn about themselves, all the while learning even more about yourself. Many people have completed multiple step studies as leaders, and each of them has learned more about themselves in each successive study.

"Choose my instruction instead of silver, knowledge rather than choice gold." (Proverbs 8:10)

"Apply your heart to instruction and your ears to words of knowledge." (Proverbs 23:12)

E—Encouragers

One of the key roles leaders play is that of encourager. From time to time, a leader will be called on to encourage others to stay on the path of recovery or to take the next step to go further down that road. You don't have to be a cheerleader to encourage people; an authentic word spoken out of love will mean so much more.

"Anxiety weighs down the heart, but a kind word cheers it up." (Proverbs 12:25)

"Therefore encourage one another and build each other up, just as in fact you are doing." (1 Thessalonians 5:11)

A—Available

Here's some good news: leaders aren't perfect; they are just available. To be a great leader, you don't have to have it all together. Because you are now completing at least your second step study, you have been in recovery a long time, and have experiences and victories to draw on that are invaluable for new participants. You don't have to have all the answers; all you have to be is available. Leaders are available to lead groups, but they are also available to have conversations—in person and over the phone—with the people they are serving. Of course, you don't have to be available *all the time*; that's one reason we have coleaders in the groups.

"Every day they continued to meet together in the temple courts. They broke bread in their homes and ate together with glad and sincere hearts." (Acts 2:46)

"Glorify the LORD with me; let us exalt his name together." (Psalm 34:3)

D—Dependable

One of the key qualities of a leader is dependability. Leaders need to be people others can count on. That *doesn't* mean leaders are responsible for others' doing the right thing or that they need to fix people. It *does* mean that they need to do what they say they are going to do. Our walks need to match our talks. When a leader promises to be somewhere, he or she needs to be there. Each week, the group is depending on the leader being present. That's not to say a leader can't miss a week now and then, but he or she needs to be there most of the time, especially for the newcomer.

"And as for you, brothers and sisters, never tire of doing what is good." (2 Thessalonians 3:13)

"Let us not become weary in doing good, for at the proper time we will reap a harvest if we do not give up." (Galatians 6:9)

"But as for you, be strong and do not give up, for your work will be rewarded." (2 Chronicles 15:7)

E—Examples

What is the best way to lead? By example. Great leaders don't tell people what to do; they show them. The best way to lead by example is to share what you have learned. That means that leaders share and follow the small group guidelines during group. Yes, we share about the victories, freedom, and hope we have found, but we are also real and open about our current struggles. By sharing in this way, we will set the example for everyone else.

"Remember your leaders, who spoke the word of God to you. Consider the outcome of their way of life and imitate their faith." (Hebrews 13:7)

Jesus said, "Now that I, your Lord and Teacher, have washed your feet, you also should wash one another's feet. I have set you an example that you should do as I have done for you." (John 13:14–15)

"Don't let anyone look down on you because you are young, but set an example for the believers in speech, in conduct, in love, in faith and in purity." (1 Timothy 4:12)

R—Relational

Leading in Celebrate Recovery is all about relationships. It's been said that "people don't care about how much you know until they know how much you care." Although leaders do have other roles, their main job is to love people. Get to know the people in your group. Learn their names; spend time with them; be open and honest with them. All of the other attributes of a leader are wrapped up into this one. This doesn't mean you have to be an extrovert or that you have to know everyone; God uses each of us differently, but loving people is a must!

"In your relationships with one another, have the same mindset as Christ Jesus." (Philippians 2:5)

"Jesus replied: 'Love the Lord your God with all your heart and with all your soul and with all your mind.' This is the first and greatest commandment. And the second is like it: 'Love your neighbor as yourself.' All the Law and the Prophets hang on these two commandments." (Matthew 22:37–40)

"And let us consider how we may spur one another on toward love and good deeds, not giving up meeting together, as some are in the habit of doing, but encouraging one another—and all the more as you see the Day approaching." (Hebrews 10:24–25)

The need for new leaders to lead open-share groups and step study groups has never been greater! It is so exciting that God is going to allow us to double the amount of step study groups with *The Journey Continues.* But that can only happen if you step across the line and become a leader, to give the same opportunities to others that you were given.

Questions for Reflection and Discussion

1. Are you ready to become a Celebrate Recovery leader? If not, what's holding you back? If yes, what steps do you need to take next?

2. Which qualities of a leader do you feel you are strongest in? How did you become strong in that area?

3. Which qualities of a leader do you see as your weakest areas? What will you do to grow in those areas?

4. What is the last lesson you learned about yourself in Celebrate Recovery? Be specific.

5. How do you show encouragement to others?

6. How do you show others you are available for them?

7. What does being a dependable leader mean to you?

8. How can you share from your experience, strength, and hope to help the people in your group?

9. What does the statement "People don't care how much you know until they know how much you care" mean to you?

10. If you are already a leader, share about the greatest joy you have experienced as a leader.

Prayer

Heavenly Father, thank You for all of the changes You have made in me. Thank You for the people and experiences You have given me in Celebrate Recovery. Now I ask You to help me give back to others in service as a leader. Show me the steps I need to take to become a Celebrate Recovery leader and help me as I take on this commitment. Thank You for placing me in a ministry that allows me to give back to You and others. In Your name I pray, amen.

Afterword

Congratulations! You have now completed *The Journey Continues!* Take a few moments to thank God for all of the things He revealed to you during this study. We hope you have learned more about yourself; found victory over your hurts, hang-ups, and habits; and, most importantly, grown closer to Jesus as a result of this study.

So what's next? There are three options. First, you can step up and lead a group of participants through the step studies you have completed. The second option is to serve in your local church. Whether you serve in Celebrate Recovery or in another ministry is up to you, but don't miss out on the opportunity of giving back to others. The third option is to go back and do another study for yourself. If you feel that you need some more time exploring your hurts, hang-ups, and habits, you may want to repeat *The Journey Continues*. All three options are win–win!

One last thing: people need to hear your story! While Celebrate Recovery is an anonymous and confidential program, each of us needs to take the courageous next step of telling others about what Jesus has done for us. That means breaking our own, but no one else's, anonymity by sharing our stories. Prayerfully consider how you can invite others to attend Celebrate Recovery with you and how you can help them begin their own recovery journey.

Here is one final acrostic to help you stay focused on the JOURNEY. By applying this acrostic daily, you will keep the journey alive!

The JOURNEY Continues

J—Jesus is the Leader

"The LORD makes firm the steps of the one who delights in him; though he may stumble, he will not fall, for the LORD upholds him with his hand." (Psalm 37:23–24)

O — Open your heart and mind to continue to seek and follow God's will

"Teach me to do your will, for you are my God; may your good Spirit lead me on level ground." (Psalm 143:10)

U — Unite with others continuously. This journey is not meant to be traveled alone.

"Therefore if you have any encouragement from being united with Christ, if any comfort from his love, if any common sharing in the Spirit, if any tenderness and compassion, then make my joy complete by being like-minded, having the same love, being one in spirit and of one mind. Do nothing out of selfish ambition or vain conceit. Rather, in humility value others above yourselves, not looking to your own interests but each of you to the interests of the others." (Philippians 2:1–4)

R — Remember your victories, but do not rest on them

"But thanks be to God! He gives us the victory through our Lord Jesus Christ. Therefore, my dear brothers and sisters, stand firm. Let nothing move you. Always give yourselves fully to the work of the Lord, because you know that your labor in the Lord is not in vain." (1 Corinthians 15:57–58)

N — Need to continue living daily in Principles 7 and 8

"Being confident of this, that he who began a good work in you will carry it on to completion until the day of Christ Jesus." (Philippians 1:6)

E—Encourage others by serving, especially the newcomer

"But encourage one another daily, as long as it is called 'Today,' so that none of you may be hardened by sin's deceitfulness."
(Hebrews 3:13)

Y—You will continue to grow in Christ to become more Christlike

"Neither do people light a lamp and put it under a bowl. Instead they put it on its stand, and it gives light to everyone in the house. In the same way, let your light shine before others, that they may see your good deeds and glorify your Father in heaven."
(Matthew 5:15–16)

We would love to hear about victories you experienced during *The Journey Continues*. Please let us know what Jesus has done for you during this study by visiting www.celebraterecovery.com/thejourneycontinues so we can celebrate with you.

John Baker
Johnny Baker

ALSO AVAILABLE

CELEBRATE RECOVERY
30
ANNIVERSARY

Celebrate Recovery®

365 DAILY DEVOTIONAL

This daily devotional is specially designed to complement the Celebrate Recovery® program. It features 366 brief original readings, each a powerful reminder of God's goodness, grace, and redemption and an inspiration to anyone struggling with old hurts, habits, and hang-ups. The *Celebrate Recovery 365 Daily Devotional* will encourage everyone who is on the road to recovery.

9780310458845

Available now at your favorite bookstore.

ZONDERVAN®

JOHN BAKER
Celebrate Recovery
JOURNAL
Celebrate Recovery JOURNAL
BAKER

ALSO AVAILABLE

CELEBRATE RECOVERY 30 ANNIVERSARY

Celebrate Recovery®

LEADER'S KIT

For over 30 years, Celebrate Recovery® has helped the church fulfill its role as Christ's healing agent. Since 1991, millions of people have participated in the Celebrate Recovery programs offered at more than 35,000 churches, prisons, and rescue missions in 21 different languages. Developed by John Baker and Rick Warren of Saddleback Church, Celebrate Recovery draws from the Beatitudes to help people overcome their hurts, hang-ups,and habits. Rather than setting up an isolated recovery community, this powerful program helps participants and their churches come together and discover new levels of care, acceptance, trust, and grace.

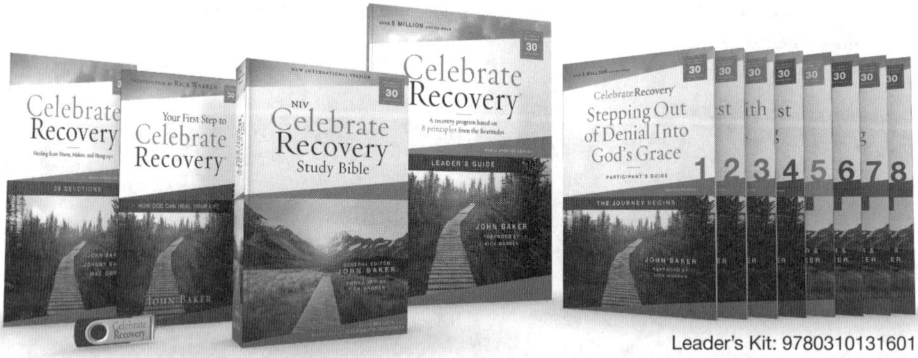

Leader's Kit: 9780310131601

The 30th anniversary leader's kit includes:

- 1 *Celebrate Recovery Leader's Guide*
- 1 each of *The Journey Begins* participant's guides #1-4
- 1 each of *The Journey Continues* participant's guides #5-8
- 1 Leader's Resource USB stick with 25 editable lessons from *The Journey Begins* curriculum, three videos featuring John Baker, Johnny Baker, and Rick Warren, sermon transcripts, and MP3 sermons.
- 1 *NIV Celebrate Recovery Study Bible*, Comfort Print® edition
- 1 copy of *Your First Step to Celebrate Recovery*
- 1 copy of *Celebrate Recovery 28 Devotions*

Available now at your favorite bookstore.

ZONDERVAN®